THE
YOUNIVERSE IN
Balance

A practical, five-step guide on
how to realign the universal elements
that result in fulfillment and a happier life.

Farzin (Frank) Kamal

ISBN-13: 978-0-9910235-1-6

Book Cover & Design by PIXEL eMarketing INC.

Legal Disclaimer

This book is dedicated to:

My parents, who left this world way too soon but managed to teach me to believe in myself and to see the inherent good in others.

Acknowledgements

I would like to express my sincerest gratitude to the many people who helped me directly or indirectly with writing this book—to all those who provided inspiration and guidance by sharing their wisdom, those who offered their point of view through discussions and those who made it possible through their assistance with the editing and the design process.

I am thankful to all the great teachers, coaches, authors, scholars, artists, philosophers, and thought leaders of the past and present who have enriched my life by sharing their wisdom. Their thoughts and observations have been instrumental in my personal growth and progress.

Special thanks go out to my wife, *Shabnam*, who supported me throughout the time it took me to bring my ideas to paper. As I struggled with making sense of what I wanted to say, she constantly encouraged me to stay committed to my inner truth and trust my intuition. For that and many other moments of inspiration, she made this book a reality.

I also want to thank my daughters, *Roxanna* and *Autash*, for being who they are—genuine, peaceful, and compassionate. Their passion for life and what they do makes our lives rich with love and happiness.

I am extremely grateful to my three wonderful brothers, my amazing sister and their families for always being there for me and for each other. The generous love that makes our bond unbreakable has been a source of inspiration and peace in my life.

I offer unconditional love and eternal gratitude to my dear aunt Parvin for being our second mom and for dedicating her life to making ours better.

Let's not forget the extended members of my family—aunts, uncles, cousins and in-laws. You are all cherished and loved by me.

My sincere appreciation goes to my very special friends. They are a constant source of joy, support, and happiness. They help fill my life with precious experiences.

Big thanks to Melissa Se and her team of editors and designers—without their support and expertise this book would never have been published. They have done a great deed by allowing me to offer my thoughts and by creating an opportunity for others to benefit from what I have humbly presented.

Finally, I offer my deepest apologies to anyone who believes they were neglected and not mentioned on these pages. Please know that I am truly grateful for everyone in my life. You are all my teachers.

FIVE STEPS TO UNIVERSAL FREEDOM

*Balance…Freedom…Happiness…Self-discovery…*These are all lifelong pursuits in the minds of all of us who want more from life than the average. I am sure you are no exception to this!

We all want to be happy and to be able to enjoy life in its entirety. But there is no magic blueprint for success, no manual that walks us through this amazing journey.

With this book, my aim is to give you a formula for realizing and living a happier life through understanding and leveraging some key universal elements available to all of us.

My name is Farzin (Frank) Kamal. I am an entrepreneur, a business consultant, a soccer coach, a part–time inventor, a certified professional life coach and now a first time author. I was born in Iran and arrived in America at the impressionable age of sixteen with the typical hopes and dreams of any young person. As is often the case with everyone's life, things did not exactly go according to plans. In what seemed to be the flash of an eye, the political unrest in my country of birth and a subsequent regime change altered the course of my life and those of my generation.

Along with my younger brother, as a 16-year-old high school student, I was cast into the world of competition, financial pressure, emotional stress, and hardship in a foreign land with nothing but the ability to learn as my strongest asset. Luckily, I also had a very supportive upbringing, and my parents instilled in me a strong sense of value that I honor to this day.

I discovered very quickly that there was immense power inside of me, an inner drive that pushed me forward. I quickly became self-sufficient and began my incredible awareness journey at that very young age.

During my years in college and my twenty-five years as an entrepreneur, I have often focused on personal growth, strong relationships, and perspective adjustments to find ways to overcome life's challenges. I nurtured sincere love for my wife through communication, compromise, and continuous learning. Together, we brought out the best in each other and managed to raise two beautiful, balanced daughters through patience, humility, support, and leading by example.

In 2004 the acquisition of the manufacturing company that I co-owned with a couple of my friends gave me the chance to explore a new path in life, and I started my consulting business. With this simple move, things started to make more sense in my life as I found harmony in helping others achieve their dreams. Little did I know that I was really realizing a lifelong purpose.

This book is not about having it all. It is about finding your own route to balance, harmony, and universal freedom by understanding key principles that may take a lifetime to discover. I began writing this book for myself, but now I know that it is meant for others. It is meant for anyone who needs to achieve clarity and a more meaningful direction to follow.

The book is about Passion, Perspective, Purpose, Planning, and Progress—and how understanding and leveraging these universal elements help keep us all in balance. These five steps, or elements, will help you find universal alignment as you get in touch with the true essence of your existence in the pursuit of a happier life. It is my hope that as they did for me, they will help guide you in your life's journey.

After all, happiness can only be achieved when you understand yourself and your YOUniverse.

STEP 1

Passion

Chapter 1

PASSIONATE LIVING

"Cherish your visions and your dreams as they are the children of your soul, the blueprints of your ultimate achievements."
NAPOLEON HILL

W hy start with passion? Because to lead a passionate life is to feel strongly about the way you live. Intense emotions often lead to action, which can help you on your journey if you leverage it in the right places.

Passion has very distinct characteristics:

- Passion is personal
- Passion has to be positive in nature
- Passion needs to be discovered
- Passion needs to be practiced

Above all, passion creates energy, and energy is what naturally flows through all of us. Without it, you cannot hope to achieve even the most simplest of things.

The Opposite of Passionate Living

Allowing the daily grind to chip away at your dreams is the opposite of passionate living. Never let life's challenges get in the way of experiencing your passion. Focus on what truly matters, and you can rise above it all. Even though events and circumstances seem to stand in your path, you will get to control how, when, where, and why simply by harnessing the energy you receive from the passions you hold dear. Passion has the ability to lift you above your circumstances. It can turn boredom into action, pain into recovery, and blockage into new ideas.

Every day there are opportunities to discover new passions in your life. Trust the drive from within, and it will serve as a tool to help balance your approach to life and its challenges. To live passionately is to surrender to this source of energy that the universe has instilled in you and to keep connected to it.

Living With Passion Is a Choice

It was prolific life coach Tony Robbins who said, "Live with passion!" Accepting and practicing this simple yet profound statement can be life changing in itself because when life naturally progresses from its carefree stages during our early years and becomes "real," most people give up on their passion. They collapse into safe mode and lose their inner child. They begin to wish for magical things to happen to them rather than creating and living the magical moment. Unlike a child, they can no longer use their imaginations to turn an old box into an Arthurian castle.

As a child, you were able to do this because passion was your dominant concern. Now you allow your main concerns to be far less dynamic—bills, work, family, drama, pets, and more bills. But Tony Robbins teaches us that it is still possible to turn everyday events into life-changing experiences. All you have to do is stop waiting and start rediscovering the passion that is locked away inside you.

There is a life out there that you want, and it is only possible if you let passion back into your everyday living. That life has not gone anywhere; it has been waiting for the passionate you!

We all have obstacles, challenges, and hardships. I have personally always realized that holding on to things that you are passionate about makes dealing with life challenges much easier. Personal fulfillment does not fall into your lap after you have settled for the life you can "manage" to live. It will only happen when passion fuels that inner fire until it is bright and hot again. Then you can use this fire to move forward and reconnect with your dreams. Seek out passion, and it will find you!

An Accurate Definition of Passion

Passion can be difficult to define, especially when you, like many adults caught in the challenges of day-to-day life, have spent years disconnecting yourself from it. But I think Oprah Winfrey said it best when she said, "Passion is energy. Feel the power that comes from focusing on what excites you."

So passion is a form of energy—a unique form of human energy that exists to help us function better in life and achieve our goals. I truly believe that passion is "soul fuel". Without it, you will run out of the food that feeds your very soul. We all need passion in our lives. It shapes our existence, inspires us, and opens our eyes to the opportunities that exist for us in everyday living.

You are in your most authentic form when passion is driving your behavior. Are you allowing enough time for things that create excitement in your everyday living? Is that what is missing in your life? A huge part of universal alignment is about leveraging the things in your life that you are passionate about. Whenever you align who you are with what you love, pure life energy is the result.

Passion also has a way of making you more courageous. Obstacles will cease to seem impossible; challenges will be met with a positive attitude.

If you do not know what you are passionate about, accept that as a challenge. A big part of life is discovering the things, people, and places that give you access to this abundant source of energy. Find a way to stay connected to this force every single day; it will bring you closer to balance, harmony, and happiness. That is more than a fact; it is an undeniable reality that is evident in those who live a passionate life.

Finding Your Personal Motivator

Passion may be hard to define at times because it often means different things to different people. One important thing to remember is that the very source of your passion comes from who you are, and we are all unique. This is what makes passion an incredibly personal thing. To an artist, passion means expression, creativity, and exposure. To an athlete, passion means hard work, discipline, and courage.

Do not expect to find your passion lying in the forgotten desk drawers of someone else's life. This is your personal motivator, and it is a journey of discovery that must be taken personally. Passion is a powerful motivator, and it is the first step to aligning who you are with what you want from this life you have been living.

Our society often associates financial success with happiness, but no amount of money automatically guarantees continuous happiness by itself. Passion, however, will definitely improve how happy you are at any given moment.

Passion is the spark that ignites the joy in life, and it should never be put to rest or packed away. Be honest. Have you sidelined your passions because of the daily grind? If so, it is time to make a change. I know it can be tough getting excited about something when you are exhausted, overworked, and underpaid. But passion can change that for you if you let it.

Committing yourself to finding your personal motivators is fun and exciting. The search will expose you to different facets of life as you attempt to identify what belongs close to your heart.

One of the Keys to Happiness

As I mentioned briefly before, passion is one of the keys to happiness. Recognizing and experiencing the things you are passionate about is instrumental in helping to put you in a happier and more productive mode. I believe happiness is a state of being created through the collection of extraordinary moments that are woven into the tapestry of our lives.

When you find and experience your true passion—or several of your true passions—happiness becomes a more regular occurrence in your life. The experiences that you have become powerful and memorable, and this makes you feel that deep internal satisfaction that many people find so difficult to grasp.

Thomas Edison used to say, *"I never did a day's work in my life. It was all fun."* Like many visionaries, Thomas was so passionate about invention that he did not consider it to be work. If you can find something you love this much—and you get to do it every day—of course you are going to be a happier person. That is how the universe works.

If instead of pursuing your passions, you did what almost everyone else does and locked them away, open that door and let happiness burst out once again.

Age and time are irrelevant when it comes to passion. You can be ten years old or sixty—it will never go away because it is part of your essence. It is part of who you are.

Once you have captured your passion and you begin to leverage it, it will become one of the most powerful things in your life. This is the key you have been waiting to receive.

The Multiple Passion Theory

People may find their source of inspiration in different places and through multiple activities at any given point in their lives. This is why it is very possible to have more than one passion during a lifetime. In fact, many people use their passion in different areas to enrich their lives with the experience of achievement, success, and happiness. A CEO may have a passion for business, but his passions for model airplanes, growing prize-winning vegetables in his greenhouse, and educating his kids are just as important in helping him achieve balance and harmony.

There is a lot of noise out there in the world on passion; what it means and how it is defined. But what you really need to know is that you can find real passion in anything positive that excites you and fills you with energy. That is what multiple passion theory is all about. Passion in your life can exist in more than one single area. If you feel enthusiasm for something, it may be a passion of yours. That is why you should never stop searching. Even if you think you have found your one true passion, there may be many others to discover in your lifetime. They will link together to form a limitless source of energy, excitement, and possibility all through your life.

With passion to guide your way, you will make progress toward universal alignment and the bliss that comes with it.

Chapter 2

DISCOVERING AND PRACTICING PASSION

"Neglecting passion blocks creative flow. When you're passionate, you're energized. Likewise, when you lack passion, your energy is low and unproductive. Energy is everything when it comes to earning."

GABRIELLE BERNSTEIN

Some of the things you may be passionate about are obvious to you. But passion can also be illusive in nature; it has to be actively identified through experience, pursued, and then practiced. This is how you attract and cultivate passion—by practicing it. Together let us explore a few levels of understanding in order to better leverage passion in our lives.

Finding Passion in What You Do for a Living

Do what you love. It is an old saying and one that tends to haunt more people than it helps. The statement, however, is not complete in my opinion. Let's reframe the saying and say, "find passion in what you do." I realize when you are stuck in a nine to five job that you do not enjoy, finding passion in what you do is the last thing on your mind. But if you try and find an aspect of your job that energizes you and gives you a sense of achievement, the job will take on a totally different meaning in your life. This is the power of finding passion.

An example of this is when my wife and I were discussing the stress of her job as a radiation therapist. She was frustrated about the sad realities of treating cancer patients on a daily basis. I encouraged her to think differently about what she does for a living and to reframe it in a positive and empowering statement. To me what she did every day was save lives and prolong family ties. I suggested that she write in bold letters "We save lives every day," post this statement in a visible place in her office, and read it whenever the stress of her job was too overwhelming. Now here is a reason to be passionate about your job!

Work is not the only passion worth pursuing. It matters a lot in life, which is why it is spoken about most often. I bet no one has ever told you that your passion does not have to be your profession!

If your one true passion is basketball but you are 5'6" with limited jumping ability and poor hand–eye coordination, then perhaps BEING a basketball player is not for you. This does not change the fact that basketball is your passion. It can still be a positive and enriching part of your life! Instead of making yourself miserable trying to be a professional basketball player, do it in your spare time.

You do not have to do your passion for a living; you just have to do it! Be an accountant who loves basketball. Go to all the games, play pickup games, and collect the memorabilia. Play on community teams and be the best at that. Your passion should always be an important part of your life. It will inspire, and in the case of the accountant, make him better at what he does because of it.

How to Discover Your Unique Passion

Passion is something each of us needs to discover over time. If you are lucky, you already know exactly what you love to do.

If you have no idea where your passion lies, that is all right as well. There are millions of people in the world who have to search in earnest to find theirs.

One thing to remember is that passion is always discovered through the experience of doing.

Discovering your passion transcends age, culture, language, and circumstances. You can do it at any time, from any location. It just takes commitment to try new things. You will have to learn to tap into your hopes and dreams and identify the parts of yourself that are enhanced when you perform certain tasks.

For example, a young woman with a hectic job may only have a handful of ideas about herself, as she has not yet discovered who she is. Every day she will dedicate some time to discovery and follow the clues her intuition lays out for her. Finally, she settles on baking! Why? Because when she bakes, she seems to get a flood of ideas and cannot wait to do it again. This is the calling card of passion, regardless of the activity.

To experience the same flow of energy and livelihood, you will also need to overcome your insecurities to find out what you really, genuinely love to do. If you do not dedicate some time in your life to enjoying your passion, you suppress part of who you are. That is why identification and attraction are crucial steps in this discovery process. Remember true passion does not die; it lasts forever.

If you have never dedicated time to discovering your true passion (or passions), it is high time you did so. They have been waiting for you!

Looking Back to Find Key Motivators

One great way to recognize or rediscover what you may be passionate about is to look back at your past experiences.

As you go through life, you experience various activities, feelings, or memories that stay with you as if an inner force inside you does not want to let them go. This can be the first clue pointing to a passion that may be lurking in your past. These are what I call your "key motivators."

To help identify these key motivators, I would recommend making a list. It does not have to be a particularly long list but one that can get you started with looking back.

When making the list, examine the times in your life when you felt happiest. Think of your triumphs and achievements, the things you were naturally good at, and the activities you could not wait to take part in. These questions can help with the process:

- What mattered most to you as a child?
- What did you love then and now?
- What were your dreams, and what are they now?
- Who did you enjoy being around?
- What do you find most beautiful in this world?
- If you had it all, what would you be doing?

Take some time to think about these questions. Do not try to answer them quickly. Give yourself a chance to tap into your past experiences and feelings. Take notes. Draw pictures on a large chalkboard—whatever stimulates your imagination. Soon your passion will reveal itself. Even if you already have a passion in mind, there may be another in your past, waiting to be discovered.

Then Hours Went Missing

There is one clear-cut way to determine whether you really enjoy doing something. It is based on the principle that time is relative to what you are actively participating in. This is why when you are bored, the day drags by, but when you do something you are passionate about, you tend to lose track of time. It feels like NO time has passed at all.

When hours go missing, you know you have tapped into something interesting…perhaps a true passion. It makes sense then to look at the things you do, that seemingly cause hours to vanish from your day.

A word of caution—losing hours in negative activities is not part of discovering your passion. Your true passion in life has to be positive in nature and must create positive energy in your life.

Ask yourself the following questions to help identify a potentially hidden passion:

- Where do you lose yourself?
- Which positive activities steal hours from your day?
- Which positive activities do you want to return to again and again?
- Do you think about the activity often?
- Do you wish you could be doing the activity all the time?

Passion is a doing word. If you are going to discover what matters most to you, you should be willing to evaluate how you spend your time. Your inner self will yearn for your passion, which will help you identify it. Just remember to keep it positive and fulfilling!

While discovering your passion, be prepared to be surprised. You may discover a passion you had not thought of before. You may find yourself taking a little longer to prepare healthy, delicious meals—could it be that cooking is a passion of yours? Anything is possible in your ongoing journey.

Focus Is Directly Related to Passion

Being able to focus on something or an activity for long periods of time is quite a keen indicator that you may have a real passion for it.

This is another tool to be aware of when trying to identify things that you may be passionate about. Focus and passion are irrevocably linked, and it is that all-encompassing and effortless focus that allows you to completely immerse yourself in the activity that you love.

Of course, some people have the ability to focus on anything because they have a passion for learning. It can be tricky if you are a naturally focused individual. But the truth usually will reveal itself. I like to call it the "extra mile" focus because you can be fairly certain it is a passion if while you are focusing, you are willing to go the extra mile on whatever it is you are working on.

When examining this, ask yourself the following questions and review the answers to help discover a seemingly hidden passion.

- Where in your life are you the most focused?

- What do you focus on?
- What is the focus like? Is it effortless?
- How do you feel when you are focused?

When the left and right sides of your brain are engaged and working together, the result is focus. The moment when you are no longer distracted, restless, or otherwise bored with what you are doing, you may be uncovering a new passion.

Focus is a combination of extreme attention, engagement, and curiosity. Discovery is a very big part of being able to focus. If it is easy for you to snap into "the zone" during an activity, you could have a passion for what you were doing.

Five Ways to Live a Passionate Life

There are many ways to live a passionate life, and doing so will greatly improve how you feel about yourself and the world.

When you begin to practice your passions on a daily basis or as often as possible, you will eventually realize they are filling your life with much needed energy, love, and enthusiasm. You can then spread these positive feelings around, which will improve everything—work, home, family, friends—everything.

Here are a five ways to live a life of passion:

1. Make time for what you love to do.
2. Never stop discovering and exploring new passions.
3. Learn all you can about your passion.
4. Use your newfound energy to offset the more boring times.
5. Inspire others to seek happiness through passion.

Discovering and practicing your passion will provide the energy you need to tackle life and its challenges. The next step is to understand how to use this energy in combination with empowering perspectives to deal with what life may have in store for you.

When passion fills your life with energy, you will begin to see paths you never knew existed. These paths can lead you to something truly great if you allow them to. How you view the world will change, and this will further enhance your goal to align who you are with what you want from life.

Universal alignment can only be achieved when the five steps have been internalized, performed, and integrated into your life.

Passion—it is personal and comes from your core. It must be discovered and practiced.

STEP 2
Perspective

Chapter 3

LIVING WITH PERSPECTIVE

"A man is but the product of his thoughts. What he thinks, he becomes."

GANDHI

Developing the right perspective is the second step on your journey to universal alignment. It involves how you see the world and everything in it. The perspective you have right now was formed over your lifetime, learned from the people around you and the experiences that you have encountered.

In the following pages we will get more into examining perspective and your choices. However, the one thing I would like you to internalize about perspective is that it has to always be positively empowering.

When One Door Closes, Another Opens

Simply put, your perspective in life dictates the actions that you take or do not take. So do you see the other open door when one closes? With the right perspective, there is always another way to solve a problem, to create harmony, or to seek synergy with others.

Your mental outlook is instrumental to aligning your life with everything the universe has to offer. It is based on many factors, it is central to your existence, and it drives your behavior. A negative perspective creates blind spots in your life causing you to lose the ability to recognize obvious opportunities.

You are what you think, and what you think is based on your outlook. Believe you are capable, and you will be. With the correct perspective driving you forward, you can turn any experience into something positive.

Advice from Thomas Edison on Perspective

Thomas Edison was considered one of the greatest inventors of his age. Not only did he invent the light bulb but he also held patents for more than 1,090 other inventions. Edison was not the kind of man who lost perspective. He knew it was an essential part of life to approach a problem step by step, even if one of those steps was a failure. He was famously quoted as saying, *"I have not failed. I've just found 10,000 ways that won't work."* Edison was talking about the light bulb, which took many times to get right.

This may sound simple, but Edison's empowering belief made it possible for him to learn and move forward instead of accepting defeat. With the right perspective, nothing stands in your way.

Unfortunately, most people are inclined to give up and wallow in their failure. But this is the easy way out. The right perspective allows for a wider view of possibilities to keep you going no matter what.

Be mindful of your point of view because in an environment without empowering perspective, failure leads to inaction. Inaction forces you to live below your potential; an unrealized potential may be the ultimate form of failure. To avoid it, universal alignment must take place!

You should be starting to see the connections between the elements we have discussed so far. Discovering and practicing your passion give you internal energy. This, in turn, will help give you a more empowering perspective about life and its infinite possibilities.

An Accurate Definition of Perspective

Perspective, simply put, is how you view things. It is the angle from which you analyze life and its circumstances. How you perceive situations will also drive your actions.

I define perspective as the driving force behind all actions that shape your personal universe.

It is also important to recognize that perspective is developed through past experiences, your personal upbringing, education, and adopted social values. Gaining the right perspective is about being conscious of your situation and then optimizing your reaction to it in a way that benefits you the most.

Perspective is a pivotal factor in your life. To better manage its impact, it helps to realize that perspective:

- Has a central and driving role in your actions.
- Is a learned behavior and can be changed.
- Is always a choice.

The world is full of negative and positive things. But that does not mean you have to react that way to them. Choosing to see things from a positive perspective is real power. You must change your perspective to improve your life. Then, as time billows by, your life will change around you for the better.

This Is Central in Your Life

"Thirty spokes of a wheel all join at a common hub yet only the hole at the center allows the wheel to spin...."
Lao Tzu *(Tao Te Ching translated by Jonathan Starr)*

The hole in the middle of the wheel may seem unimportant, but change its shape and the wheel will not function properly. Perspective is central to your life in the same way. It is the driving force behind all of your actions and behaviors. It is also the single most impactful thing to change about you.

Learn to work on the way you perceive the things around you. Question your perspectives. Do not automatically accept them as the truth. If you can improve the way you perceive things, everything around you will respond with improvement as well. Imagine yourself in a hotel at night. You look out the window and only darkness stares back. You feel safe in your room, like the world is continuing inside and not outside. In the morning, you look out that same window. People are bustling by, going about their daily functions. You realize that you were never alone. The only thing that changed was your perspective.

Success cannot be achieved by people who do not leverage the central role of their perspectives. Because they are central to your life, they will dictate your actions, and only the right actions will lead to success.

What Can Be Learned Can Be Changed

"To improve is to change; to be perfect is to change often."
Winston Churchill

Your perspectives are often results of learned behaviors. As you click along on life's grand journey, the people you meet influence your perspectives in subtle ways. The process begins as you absorb values, experiences, and education from multiple sources. These are the things you learn from parents, friends, family, teachers, and your social environment. This then moves into your belief system, where your inner self controls your pain and fear responses as well as your pleasure and desire triggers. This swiftly projects itself out as your perspective—or what you seemingly can and cannot do.

The final stage in the process is the action phase, where negative and positive behaviors control your life and how you get to live it. However, anything that can be learned can be unlearned or changed. Even though these learned behaviors have become part of your belief system, you can take steps to consciously change how you see things.

This starts by getting to know you.

According to Lao Tzu, a wise Chinese philosopher known as the father of Taoism,

> *"Knowing others is intelligence; knowing yourself is true wisdom. Mastering others is strength; mastering yourself is true power."*
> (Tao Te Ching translated by Jonathan Starr)

When you have power over your perspectives, everything in life becomes easier. By making a conscious choice to understand you and to choose the path that leads to success, you become better equipped to discover your life's purpose.

It is up to you to change the cycles that have made it impossible for you to rise above your circumstances and achieve your dreams. Life experience may teach you how you think you should be, but these are narrow, limited thought processes. Unleash your potential by moving away from these shackles.

Working with Choice

> *"When you have to make a choice and don't make it, that is in itself a choice."*
> William James

Choice is one of the things that separates us from animals and puts us in charge of our own destiny. The difference between you and a lion is that besides basic instincts, you are also able to exercise free will.

Interestingly enough, choice is also the reason why so many of us live hollow, meaningless, and subpar lives. By not making the right choice, you inadvertently affect your life in a negative manner. Your perspective is a choice as well. Even though you may not have realized it until now, you have been the master of your own fate all along.

Your previous childhood programming and experiences have forced you to view life in a way that you may not be happy about. Well, I would like to interrupt your regular programming for a special message! You are in charge of yourself!

Beliefs and behaviors are choices. You have been on autopilot for too long, and it's now time to take back control and switch to manual.

You have the power to make decisions that will benefit the person you are and the one you are trying to become. I will show you how to be aware of this in your life.

As an adult, you can reassess your education and take steps to correct it. With enough conscious practice, your choices will become beneficial. You will learn that you cannot control the direction of the wind but you can certainly adjust your sails.

Understanding and developing empowering perspectives is the goal that you have to pursue in this section. There is no hope trying to succeed in a world without an enabling point of view.

The right perspectives will help you bounce back from hardship and will keep you rolling forward toward universal alignment and success.

Chapter 4

UNDERSTANDING AND OPTIMIZING PERSPECTIVE

"We can complain because rose bushes have thorns, or rejoice because thorn bushes have roses."
ABRAHAM LINCOLN

To understand and optimize perspective, you need to start on a personal self-discovery journey that will take you inside yourself to where and how your thoughts interact with each other to drive your actions. Knowing how to practice seeing the world from the right perspective is a life skill you will always value.

The one fact about perspective I want you to remember is it is something that must be optimized for positive empowerment. Your beliefs must evolve until you can clearly see that your perspective on things empowers you in a positive manner.

The Five Essential Perspectives

In the realm of perspective, there are five key areas that will affect you in your life. These areas need to be looked at, examined, internalized, and then refreshed so that you can see yourself and your life within a larger context.

Empowerment comes from experience and knowing where positive thoughts will have the greatest impact. This can only be achieved if you learn to optimize your perspective in these five areas. Think of yourself as the center of a circle divided into five even sections—a 360 degree thinking wheel.

The five areas that we are going to talk about are:

1. Universal Perspective

2. Self-Perspective

3. Perspective about Others

4. Perspective of Events and Circumstances

5. Perspective about Money and Worldly Possessions

By developing empowering perspectives in these areas, you will move toward becoming a multiple perspective critical thinker, and that is a great asset in helping you choose the right actions. The right perspective also helps blur the lines between labeling results as failures or successes, creating a functional environment where all outcomes are leveraged to move forward.

Fostering Universal Perspectives

Gandhi once said, *"When I admire the wonders of a sunset or the beauty of the moon, my soul expands in the worship of the creator."*

The first of the multiple perspectives is your Universal perspective. Have you ever stopped to ask yourself how you view the universe and everyone in it? You might not think so, but this is a very foundational step in your alignment process.

You are part of a greater existence; it is you, and you are it. If you focus closely, you will see that it is there to provide for you, if only you consciously contribute to it. There is more to you than your physical body.

Some theorists believe that because of our eternal souls, we are able to connect to the universe and everything inside it. The universal consciousness, as it is called, connects us all to God, nature, space, and all of the other powerful elements in our world and beyond it.

Science cannot explain the existence of our souls or the mysterious "inner life" we all seem to live concurrently while making our way through the external world. When you see yourself as part of something greater, it certainly puts life into context.

Einstein said that "everything is energy," and energy connects us all to the limitless universe. If there is just one consciousness in the world, then we are each a small part of it. Some experts call it a "higher intelligence," and it has empowered many people to refocus their lives on what really matters—balance, prosperity, and happiness.

How do you see the world? Do you believe in a world of abundance that is governed by the universal laws that you can connect to through your personal spirituality?

Accept this mysterious higher level of existence by developing an empowering perspective that it is there and it is aware. Everything else will come into a much sharper focus.

Developing Inner Perspectives

"We must not allow other people's limited perceptions to define us."
Virginia Satir

Once you consider that you are part of a greater universe with a purpose and a plan for each of us, the rest of the perspective steps are fairly straight forward.

To develop the right inner perspectives, you need to become hyperaware of yourself and the people around you. Self-recognition is instrumental to realigning your perspectives. You are more than your job, your title, and the sum of your worldly possessions.

You are more than a dad, a mom, a sister, a brother, or a friend. You are a unique, powerful force of nature—perhaps the most perfect force in nature ever created. Inside you is a life force, known in Eastern philosophy as "chi," and it is found in everything. Many scientists have called this energy the building block of all matter and creation—physical and non-physical. Chi flows in and around us all the time. It is part of the Yin and Yang cycle of balance.

Understanding and believing that you matter just as much as anyone or anything else in the Universe is a key to developing a strong sense of self.

Recognize that you have the control. The power to change your habits has always been yours. In his book, *Think and Grow Rich*, Napoleon Hill speaks of "autosuggestion," or influencing your subconscious mind to be aligned with your conscious goals.

Write empowering statements about yourself, and be grateful for your abilities. Review them on a daily basis until they become second nature to the way you think of yourself. With enough time and dedication to the process, these new perspectives will challenge your behavior and self-confidence level. You will shine as who you really are—an amazing wonder of nature capable of limitless possibilities.

Working on How You Perceive Others

"You must not lose faith in humanity. Humanity is an ocean; if a few drops of the ocean are dirty, the ocean does not become dirty."
Gandhi

My personal perspective about others is that there is inherent good in everyone in the world, and by aligning ourselves with one another's positive energy, we can achieve things beyond our wildest imagination.

By believing there is a collective source of being that includes everything in existence, it is easy to see that our "chi" or life forces are connected. When we begin to use them properly, we are able to develop inner perspectives that allow us to feel like we are part of the world. That sense of isolation falls away, and you get back in touch with what everyone's role can be.

Most people only see others in a superficial sense, but our perception of others directly leads to the reactions we have toward them. As an enlightened person, you need to keep these in check. After all, you are connected to the people you meet. When you recognize that everyone is a force of nature when focused on the right things, this gives you power. One person can start a change that affects the world.

Imagine how knowing that everyone has this power gives you access to unlimited energies and momentums you can leverage in your life. You already know people exist in the world; now understand that they can all be additional sources of energy for you and vice versa.

Let's assume that each one of us has an energy level of 1. Opening up to others and aligning your energy with just one more person will lead to double the energy level (1+1=2). The opposite will yield a disastrous result. When you fail to align your thoughts and energy with others, you will often end up with (1-1=0). Where there is struggle for power, power is actually lost.

Empower yourself with a perspective that all the people in your life have an effect on your energy. Seek out and surround yourself with the individuals who live with a positive outlook on life and its possibilities. Together you can reach greater heights of success.

Perspective of Events and Circumstances

"In my country, we go to prison first and then become President."
Nelson Mandela

What a powerful outlook from Nelson Mandela, who was imprisoned for more than twenty-five years before becoming the president of South Africa and changing that country forever.

I always marvel at how quickly people give in to defeat and believe in having no way out. I can only assume people do this because they have a lack of understanding about the role of events in their lives.

Every day you encounter new events, new experiences, and new opportunities. An enlightened person does not see positive or negative experiences, only opportunities to succeed or opportunities to learn. Failure is often viewed as perhaps the worst thing that could ever happen to you. The truth is there can be no success without it! Failure is an essential stepping stone on the cobbled pathway to success and freedom.

Life will never stop coming at you. Challenges and obstacles exist because we do not fully understand them. Once they have been understood, they vanish. It is your job to live life to its fullest, to embrace all experiences and events to help you form an empowering perspective environment for your life.

Your circumstances are simply the sum of the lessons you have learned and internalized.

Use failed attempts to learn what does not work and create an attitude of resilience. On the other hand, once you gain success, it is equally as important that you remain humble about it. Success is an indication that you have sought out knowledge, overcome obstacles, and made your perspectives work for you. That is why we all admire it!

Creating the perspective in which failure leads to resilience and success leads to humility is an incredibly empowering and enabling environment.

Money and Material Perspectives

"Be thankful for what you have; you'll end up having more. If you concentrate on what you don't have, you will never, ever have enough."
Oprah Winfrey

You were born to a world that has everything you need to be happy. Then it changed, and your view of the material world was reshaped based on your experiences and perhaps according to a few influential people's ideals. In our modern world, money and material possessions do promote that you are successful, but they are never the end goal of success.

Money, for example, is a means for acquisition—a tool to allow you to have greater and more complex experiences in the world. It is not meant to be hoarded, or guarded, or treated as some kind of treasure.

At the end, money itself is just paper. It is what money can get you—choices—that matters; things like new experiences, buying new things, travelling, and starting new ventures. Yet people become locked in a specific "lifestyle" so much that they forget their worldly possessions are for living! We were never meant to be physically or spiritually stationary in one place for years on end. Money provides us the ability to move, share, and experience life.

Modern society quickly teaches us to treat money like some golden fleece that we need to handle with extreme reverence and admiration. The admiration should never be, "Wow, he has a lot of money," but "Wow, look at the difference he has made with his money." What positive thing have you done with your money lately?

You see, money and material possessions are a means to an end; they are not the end. You should be grateful for what you have and fully experience all you can every day so that money, much like other tools, comes to you and can be used toward your passion, purpose, and goals in life.

You can develop an empowering perspective about money and worldly possessions by being grateful for what you have and detaching your self-worth from money and viewing it as a tool. Once you do this, you will then be able to put your money to good use—in the pursuit of balance, happiness, and success. That is what you want in the first place!

Perspective: It is central to all of your actions. It must be understood and optimized for positive empowerment.

STEP 3
Purpose

Chapter 5

A PURPOSE FUELED LIFE

"Your work is to discover your world and then with all your heart give yourself to it."
GAUTAMA BUDDHA

The next step on your path to gaining universal alignment is to use the lessons you have learned about passion and perspective to find your innermost purpose. As connected individuals, we all have a role to play in this world. We just need to find it.

I strongly believe that each and every one of us has a purpose greater than ourselves is waiting for us, a purpose that must be acknowledged and recognized for us to achieve true ultimate happiness. The challenge is that our purpose in life is not always clearly obvious to us.

Gratefully Living for Each Day Now

"I was a boy when I first realized that the fullest life livable was a Poet's."
Wilfred Owen

I believe it is extremely detrimental to our sense of direction to identify our own "grand" purpose in life. Your life-long purpose, however, may be hidden in an unrealized experience—an experience that may only be possible if you live your life to the fullest while adopting an attitude of gratitude.

What if I told you that reaching for some huge "purpose" in life actually distracts you from finding your purpose? When there is something bigger to look forward to, who cares about what is happening now, right? That is a common problem here. You will never discover your real purpose in life if you are not living every day to its maximum potential with a grateful attitude. Most people allow monotony to set in. They forget to appreciate what they have and what their current life is giving them. That is one reason why their purpose evades them.

Start living a grateful day and experience each moment with gratitude. Do not look past all the subtle indications and opportunities to discover more about who you are by interacting with the world gratefully. Do not waste precious time by "waiting" for your purpose to appear; instead, actively seek it out by opening your heart and mind to the everyday wonder around you.

Nelson Mandela and Albert Einstein on Purpose

There are two big lessons about purpose that you can learn with the help of two of my greatest heroes—Nelson Mandela and Albert Einstein. Both found their purpose after enduring serious trials and tribulations in life.

Mr. Mandela said *"There is no passion to be found playing small—in settling for a life that is less than the one you are capable of living."* The great anti-apartheid hero meant that if we feel inside we are capable of doing more or being more, that is the direction we should take ourselves.

Real purpose is not a prize that waits for us at the end of a mountain climb. All you will discover once you get to the top are more mountains with more climbing ahead of you. Purpose is to know which mountain to choose to optimize the life experiences you are meant to have.

Albert Einstein speaks about purpose in his famous essay, "The World as I See It." He goes on to talk about how important deeper reflection is so that we can learn about ourselves and the people in our lives. According to Einstein, people are intrinsically part of your purpose, and we all help each other to reach our end goals.

The lessons are:

- Do not settle for a life that is less than the one you can live.

- Reflect deeply on yourself and the people in your life as they move you forward.

Purpose, while a very personal thing, is inevitably a concern for all of us. Because we are all connected, we all play our part in either helping or hindering the purpose of others. If you never give up on finding your purpose and you commit to helping others find theirs when the opportunity arises, happiness is more likely to find you.

Accurate Definition of Purpose

"My life is my message." Gandhi

Purpose can be defined as the reason something is done or for which something exists. Ultimately, we all want to understand why we exist in this world as we are. What did we come here to do? Is there a reason for the things we go through?

People often call it your "mission" or "calling" in life. In my opinion, your purpose in life is the universe's core reason for your existence in relation to all other things that exist. I believe we are all responsible for leaving this world in a better shape than when we came into it. Our contribution need not be of huge scale, but it must always be positive in nature.

Stephen Covey, author of the amazing book, *7 Habits of Highly Effective People*, suggested that a good way to hone in on your purpose is to use imagery to do it. Imagine that you have died. What do you want your tombstone to say? What is it that you would like to be remembered for? These are questions of legacy, and they will help you discover what your purpose may be in this world.

Purpose is a very personal thing, but its true nature always involves the benefit of other people around us. If you are struggling to discover your true direction, try meeting new people. Different spirits can result in new energy being brought into your life with positive outcomes.

Remember that purpose is not one particular milestone to reach. It is not a project, a career, or a moment in time. It consists of a collection of mindful experiences over time that results in your legacy—what you are going to leave behind in the world. Now let's dig a little deeper into the characteristics of purpose.

Tapping into the Higher Power

"We are more closely connected to the invisible than to the visible."
Novalis

One of the main characteristics of purpose is its ability to connect you to a higher power. You will know when you reach this place because it makes whatever you are doing at that moment completely effortless, like you are simply the vessel and what is coming out of you comes from a deeper place than our physical world.

There is a phenomenon that many artists, writers, and athletes talk about, where during their average work day or performance, they hit a "flow" or "zone," where what comes out of them does not seem to involve conscious thought or process. It simply flows from them, as if they have connected with something bigger than themselves.

You can call this source God, Allah, Tao, Nature, or the Universe, but whatever you relate it to, know that it comes from a plane that is beyond our physical world. To find your true purpose in life, you need to be aware of this level of connection.

Is there ever a time when you feel connected, closer to "God," or like you are in the right place, doing the right thing? Tapping into a higher power should be a characteristic that you actively pursue in your daily life.

By being mindful of characteristics like this, you will inch toward discovering your true purpose in life. You will know it when you feel it. It is the easiest thing in the world, and even as you are engaged in it, you wonder how it can be so fulfilling and so easy.

I believe through discovering and living our purpose, we are all able to reach this state, to harness the enormous power of the universe so that we can achieve levels of consciousness far beyond our current understanding.

Purpose within the Purpose Theory

"The purpose of life is to contribute in some way to making things better."
Robert F. Kennedy

I believe our individual purpose in life can also be defined as our specific role within the greater collective purpose of all that exists—a purpose within the purpose, if you will.

There are many theories on whether the universe itself has a purpose or not. This question has proven much too difficult for our minds to answer. However, I do believe our purpose in life as a collective unit boils down to one simple truth, and that is for us to make a positive impact on our universe during our existence as we know it. If we take this statement to be true, all we have to do is to figure out what our individual role is in the big scheme of things.

Trying to pinpoint your ultimate purpose means exploring areas that may lead up toward this far simpler and far greater overall purpose. For example, a musician can make the world a more enjoyable place by pursuing her purpose in life to make music. For a teacher, it will be to teach, and for a healer, it will be to heal. Regardless of their roles, they are all helping make a positive impact on the universe in their own way.

Purpose is usually considered to be quite unique to the individual, even though—as I have explained—it may be unique at a personal

43

level, but it certainly fits within a greater collective quest to make the world a better place.

The bottom line is even if we have difficulty really knowing what our individual purpose is, it is important to do the best with what we are given. We should strive to make a positive difference—to live, love, and really embrace the experiences life gives us. This way, no matter what, you will always contribute to the greater collective purpose of all of us.

Learn with an Open Mind to Stay Focused

"Live as if you were to die tomorrow. Learn as if you were to live forever."
Gandhi

You have grown up developing your own special set of beliefs and values based on your life experiences. When these values and beliefs stop being challenged and stop growing, they may affect your ability to stay focused on your purpose in life.

People who do not keep an open mind cannot or will not entertain the idea that things in life are not set—they continue to change. They cling to their old beliefs and values even as the world changes around them. This could lead to unhappiness and losing their sense of purpose.

It is a universal truth—change happens. It happens to you, to your family, your friends, the town where you live, and the country you live in. Even the earth changes every second of the day. An open-minded people embrace change and adapt to it—allowing the lessons that follow to help shape and guide their futures and serve their purposes.

You need to be an open-minded person to live your purpose. It is the only way you will continue along the right paths, changing with your experiences for the better.

Never allow events and circumstances to take your purpose from you. Keep moving toward it, whatever happens!

44

Chapter 6

RECOGNIZING AND EMBRACING PURPOSE

"When you dance, your purpose is not to get to a certain place on the floor. It's to enjoy each step along the way."
WAYNE DYER

In order to recognize and embrace your purpose, you will need to come to the realization that living your purpose, like dancing, is a process. A dance is not made great at the end but from the very beginning. That is why you need to learn to live a purpose-fuelled life. If you have always struggled to determine where and what you want to do in your life, you have not had the right kind of experiences yet. Get out there and get busy. Until now you have been a raft floating in a sea of options. It is time to find your island paradise!

Recognizing Your Purpose—The Characteristics

One way to help you find your purpose in life is to practice writing a personal purpose statement, also known as a personal mission statement. You can start by answering the following questions to help you create your first mission statement:

- What activity, work or non-work related, brings you the most satisfaction?
- What attracts you, engages you, and fires up your heart?
- Why do you do what you do every day?
- What legacy do you want to leave behind?

As you think about these questions, try to bring the answers to their simplest form by really squeezing the essence of your thoughts behind your answers. This process should result in a true mission statement or a life-long purpose that contains these four characteristics:

- A life purpose must serve the "greater good."
- It is always about more than just you.
- It has no time limits.
- It is never about money and material things.

These characteristics are not mutually exclusive. As a matter of fact, they must all be present simultaneously in your purpose. Examine your mission statement carefully, and if it does not have all these elements, revise it. You still have work to do.

Now let's explore these characteristics to better understand their role in shaping your purpose in life.

The Greater Good in Purpose

"For the good of the many, for the happiness of the many, out of compassion for the world."

Gautama Buddha

An important characteristic of a life purpose is that it should always be positive in nature. If your purpose contains even the slightest chance of bringing harm to all that exist in our universe, it will not serve you well and will ultimately lead to your own unhappiness.

This may sound a bit spiritual, but I have heard just about every debate possible on how people can achieve real happiness in their lives.

To date, the closest I have ever come is when the subject broached our purpose in life and how there is spiritual good in purpose. Modern life often makes us cast aside our spirituality for a more physical kind of existence, but this does not mean our spirits are any less important in our lives. We know they exist, and surely they must exist for a reason.

Purpose is for the "good" in the world. It has a positive impact and acts like a guiding light in your life that ensures what you do will be for the benefit of all mankind and the universe. For centuries, "doing good" has been seen as a natural anti-depressant.

It is no wonder that people who do good for others are often very happy people. Doing good in the context of fulfilling your life's purpose is perhaps the purest form of happiness there is in the world. That is why you should move toward it as often as you can.

A Single Universal Truth

"Only a life lived for others is a life worthwhile."
Albert Einstein

The second characteristic that will help you unearth your purpose is that purpose is universal. What does that mean? It means that your purpose starts inside you, but it is always about more than you alone.

Your true purpose in life does not just serve you; it involves the role you have to play in relation to the "bigger" purpose we all have. The universe is mysteriously an unselfish place. While a lot goes on there, with constant change and growth, it always keeps its connected nature and gives us a mirror into our lives.

Your purpose can start in connection to your family, and if it is meant to, it can grow to affect your community, your world, and the entire universe around it. Even the smallest changes can have the largest effects.

Your mission statement should always be about more than just you. I believe that life purpose starts at a personal level for every individual, and then it has the potential to blossom into a much broader force. If you want to find your place in this world, you need to be mindful of this universal truth that we are all here as connected beings.

To what and whom in the world would you like to contribute in a positive manner?

This question takes the notion of purpose and really gives you something to think about. What if I told you that inside you right now is the power to improve everyone's lives in the world for the better? Would you work harder? Each of us has a calling, and that calling leaves a space in our hearts. Until we find it, we will always feel like we are lost. Embracing your purpose fills this gap and invites you to affect the lives of others in a positive way for the good of mankind.

The Infinite Nature of Purpose

"We must use time wisely and forever realize that the time is always ripe to do right."
Nelson Mandela

Some people know who they are and what their purpose is from a young age while others barely find theirs in their later years. Time is something that never ceases, and it creates the framework for logic in our world. Purpose defies this order.

The good news is that purpose is timeless. It has no time limits in your life. You are given your entire existence to discover what your purpose may be. Some people are lucky and find it at age ten; others only discover it at age seventy. Its discovery and recognition are completely individualized.

Your purpose will last from the time you discover it through your entire life on this earth. That is why it is about HOW you live your life right now. It is not about what you do until certain goals are achieved. Life happens every day regardless of whether we are ready for it or not.

What this means is that your mission or purpose statement should not have a time limit attached to it. This is another major characteristic of a true life-long purpose. For example, if your life purpose is to help deprived children work their way out of poverty, it is not just for a day or a year; it is forever. Your level of activity may change from time to time, but your purpose is not limited by time.

The real test is making full use of every day to reach your full potential and to do as much as you can. Your talent, your drive, and your abilities did not come from nowhere. They were given to you for a reason. While we may not fully understand that reason, one thing is clear—people are happiest when they feel as though they are fulfilling their purpose in life. If you have yet to discover yours, there is still time. Lots of time!

- What would you still do if you had one day to live?
- What would you do if you were given an immortal life?

Think about these questions, and answer them truthfully. You may just unlock an unrealized path to do good in this world.

Money Matters—Or Does It?

"To understand the limitation of things, desire them."
(Tao Te Ching translated by Jonathan Starr)

Another of the key characteristics of purpose is that it is moneyless. It has no monetary nature and is beyond worldly possessions and "stuff." The definition of success has definitely been distorted over the years to mean "money."

Let us get something clear—success has nothing to do with money. If you think it does, you are reading the wrong book. Success is directly related to happiness. You can have very little money and still be a hugely successful person. That is because success really is defined as the ability to achieve your purpose in life. It is true that often when you achieve your purpose, you tend to earn more money, but by no means is it a benchmark of success.

If happiness is a side effect of helping others by achieving your purpose, then so is money. The ultimate goal, however, is to be fulfilled, to feel connected, and to have others perceive you with a sense of respect because you do good in this world.

If money did not exist on this earth, what would you be doing?

Remember that the direct pursuit of wealth has no place in your mission statement. Instead, focus on finding your purpose and on living your life to its fullest each and every day without direct focus on material goods. If you succeed, money will come.

Everyone wants to achieve wealth, but wealth does not make you happy or fulfilled. Universal alignment is about getting back in touch with your reasons for living the life you lead and embracing a better way so that you can move forward toward true success of living your life's purpose.

Embracing Your Purpose

"True happiness…is not attained through self-gratification, but through fidelity to a worthy purpose."
Helen Keller

In order to embrace your purpose, you need to embrace your life and accept that within you, you have everything to fulfill your purpose. Stop thinking about it as lacking—"I do not have X, and I still need to achieve Y." This is irrelevant, and it limits your progressions toward your ultimate purpose. Instead, embrace your life and enjoy it. Take every chance to expand it! Get out there and see where this mysterious and dynamic world takes you. You will not find your purpose being isolated from the world. The tools are available to you, but you have to plant the garden!

Once you have embraced your life as it is now, you will see that opportunities start arriving at your door thick and fast! Choose your opportunities wisely. Investigate areas you find fascinating, start new ventures, leave your comfort zone, learn, learn, and learn! It is through this process that you can sharpen your skills and remain faithful to your purpose.

Life is not only about finding your purpose; it is about fulfilling it—and that requires a journey of self-discovery and skill building. Your life will teach you what you need to know, but you have to live it first!

There will be a moment—a defining moment—when everything feels right. This is an indication that you are on the right path to finding your purpose.

Embrace your purpose when you find it, remain true to its nature and stay committed to fulfilling it every step of the way.

STEP 4
Planning

Chapter 7

A PLAN TODAY IS A GIFT TOMORROW

"Give me six hours to chop down a tree and I will spend the first four sharpening the axe."

ABRAHAM LINCOLN

When you have discovered your passion, realigned your perspective, and recognized your purpose, the next logical step forward is to develop a plan that will help guide you toward achieving your goals in life.

Although there are no guarantees that what you expect to happen is what actually happens, proper planning dramatically increases your odds of success. It is about preparing for what you think might take place even if turns out to be a small portion of the unknown future.

Living on the Wild Side

"By failing to prepare, you are preparing to fail."

Benjamin Franklin

Have you ever heard the saying *"A plan today is a gift tomorrow"*? It means when you sit down and create written plans that you track and execute to their completion, you will receive the rewards of that planning in the future. What many people do not understand is that when you do not plan, you are leaving success completely in the hands of chance.

When you do not plan at all, you are choosing to "live on the wild side." This may be fine for when you are trying a new experience or reaching for something outside the norm. However, conventional wisdom shows us that not planning for what we know is coming or what we would like to achieve usually leads to a less than optimal outcome.

Lao Tzu and Gandhi on Planning

There is an abundance of advice from various sources on the merits of planning and how important it is in achieving anything worthwhile in this world. Two of my favorite thoughts are from Lao Tzu and Gandhi. These great teachers shared valuable lessons with us—lessons that continue to hold true.

When planning, Lao Tzu told us to *"anticipate the difficult by managing the easy."* Tasks come at us in life whether we embrace them or not. Often we leave them to grow silently from small matters into large problems. The wisdom here is on prioritization—do what you must today. Clear away the work, the tasks, and the little things that may barely matter. Then you will have time for bigger things. But when you allow the little things to stack up, they become the big things that you have to deal with.

Gandhi said, *"Man falls from the pursuit of the ideal of plain living and high thinking the moment he wants to multiply his daily wants. Man's happiness really lies in contentment."* Gandhi's lesson has to do with importance of perspective in planning. He hints that man is able to naturally plan his life, but things derail when his wants get out of control.

In our modern society, we exist in a busy "want" culture, where everything seems chaotic and up for grabs if you can afford it. Lack of much needed prioritization and mindful perspectives distract people off their life path, and they fail to truly live their purpose.

An Accurate Definition of Planning

What is planning? Simply put, planning involves two elements—an end goal and the process required to meet that end goal. The idea is to map the required actions systematically and down to their most basic parts so achievement becomes easier. However, there is also the unavoidable element of "change" that may require you to be flexible and adjust your approach from time to time.

Considering the above, I define planning as a fluid map of actions—a map because it provides you with direction and fluid because it requires you to remain flexible while going through your journey. Planning needs to be flexible enough to work within the context of the unexpected eventualities that will crop up. By setting the goals you want to reach within a flexible context, your chances at success are much higher.

Planning can be a powerful tool for achieving your goals, but many people are unaware of its innate potential. They remain completely inactive when it comes to planning for their purpose-filled future. Instead, they carry on without specific goals and try to achieve with very little success.

True happiness comes with balance, and balance can be achieved when you align all five elements mentioned in this book with who you are. The planning element allows you to create a process to help guide you through this balancing act.

Action Is the Engine of Experience

"Action is the real measure of intelligence."
Napoleon Hill

There are big plans, small plans, simple plans, and complicated plans. But there are basically no plans in absence of action. What are your chances of succeeding without taking action?

Throughout this book, I talk about the importance of experiencing new activities. I have pointed out how being open to new possibilities will help you discover unrealized passions, develop empowering perspectives, and recognize a hidden life-long purpose. Now let's examine the role of action and its cycle in this mix.

Action is the engine of experience, and with the right perspective, all experiences are successful. Success fuels self-confidence and self-worth. In turn, this generates more actions and experiences. Ultimately, this cycle helps you realize your potential and prepares you for a much more balanced life.

Action is an essential part of the planning process. You may even decide to wait and not take any action as part of your plan, which in reality is an action in itself. It may be obvious, but it is only through a conscious decision of doing or not doing that results reveal themselves and planning takes shape.

The alignment of the five elements helps you create a balanced environment where taking the right action becomes second nature to you.

Letting the Mud Settle

"Do you have the patience to wait, till your mud settles and the water is clear? Can you remain unmoving till the right action arises by itself?"
Lao Tzu

When we discuss the importance of taking action in life, we also need to be mindful of the fact that the universe takes care of itself as well. Rushing into action could make things worse, and sometimes the best thing to do is sit back and let clarity take place before we act. This is what Lao Tzu calls "letting the mud settle."

I briefly mentioned non action as a form of action in the last section. This concept, called Wu Wei in Chinese, or the act of non doing, is one of the most fascinating concepts in the ancient teachings of Taoism. The concept is explored throughout various chapters of Tao Te Ching, the great Taoist guide. The concept basically encourages us to trust nature, practice patience, not force our actions, and make our decisions consciously.

During your incredible alignment journey, there will be times when you have to practice non action in its different forms as a part of your plan. For example, you could be patient and give a project or a person enough time to be successful, withdraw yourself from a tense situation before commenting, or just continue on your path without concerning yourself with what others may think.

Wu Wei, or non action, is a perfectly acceptable plan as long as your planning process is in tune with your life-long purpose, passions, and perspectives.

The Alignment Process

Planning different areas of your life cannot be a disconnected activity from the other elements you have learned about in this book. If you are going to succeed at planning, the process needs to be aligned with your passion, perspective, and purpose.

We will examine the role of goal setting in the planning process in detail in the next chapter. However, for now, let's understand that any meaningful and aligned plan has to contain these key features involving the other elements.

- It leverages your passion as a source of energy.
- It employs your positively empowering perspectives.
- It helps get you closer to living your life-long purpose.

Let's take a quick look at the goal setting process to better understand the connections between the elements. First, you have to create a goal to achieve an end point. For you to remain motivated, that end point cannot be in conflict with your ultimate purpose in life. In order to come up with a workable action plan, you have to be able to manage things as they are and as they could be. This will undoubtedly test your perspectives. Throughout all of this, you will need passion to energize you and keep you moving forward.

Mindful practice of these elements will take you toward universal alignment. Once you have made this a regular part of your life, you will find that everything begins to go more smoothly in your life. This is because you are focusing on the right parts of yourself to fuel your existence.

Chapter 8

PLANNING WITH PURPOSE

"Set your mind on a definite goal and observe how quickly the world stands aside to let you pass."
NAPOLEON HILL

We plan because we recognize we have a purpose in life. Acknowledging that things never remain the same, we plan to demonstrate our intentions in life. This is why we must learn to plan with purpose. When we focus our minds on achieving specific goals that are aligned with the greater good, the world around us responds by removing the obstacles.

The Conscious Nature of Planning

Planning is a very mindful, conscious process; it is an attempt to try and harmonize our energy and our intentions with the entire universe. All plans need to be worked on in a conscious manner. You have to be aware of your situation, the resources at your disposal, and other fundamental elements that will affect the outcomes—namely your passion, purpose, and perspective.

Your ability to align these elements using your awareness and your will is the greatest asset that you have as a life-planner. The more you use this ability to plan different parts of your life, the better you become.

Now that we have discussed the mind-set behind planning, let's examine an overview of the five steps in the actual planning process. No matter what areas of life you may be working on, these steps remain the same.

1. Get real: Where are you now?
2. Imagine a vision: Set long-term goals.
3. Break it down: Set short-term goals.
4. Start the journey: Turn action into habit.
5. Evaluate: Do more of what works, and change what does not.

Get Real: Where Are We Now?

"It's impossible to map out a route to your destination if you don't know where you're starting from."
Suze Orman

As you may recall, I defined planning as a fluid map of actions—fluid because it had to flexible and a map because it gave you direction.

Now I am sure you have seen the "You are here" labels on maps and directories to help you find your way. In the same fashion, the first step of the planning process is when you figure out where you are. The only way is to begin with this orientation. Be honest—brutally honest—and do not leave out any of the relevant bits—good or bad. Be as specific as you can so that you can get your plan off on the right foot when you begin.

Ask yourself where you are right now in life and what your current situation is. What is working, and what is not? How far along have you come? By gaining an accurate understanding of where you are now, you have your real starting point for your first real plan. Sit down and write this out. Writing is very therapeutic in that it helps get those thoughts out of your head and down on paper, where they can be reflected upon.

Imagine a Vision: Set Long-term Goals

"Imagination is everything. It is the preview of life's coming attractions."
Albert Einstein

Unlike a life-long purpose or your mission, specific plans have an end point associated with them. The next step in the planning process is to paint the big picture of these end points and to imagine a destination for each action plan. In the planning process, this is often called creating a vision or setting long-term goals. Of course, as we established, the end result of all actions should be aligned with getting you closer to living your life-long purpose.

Setting long-term goals is about looking into the future, usually one to five years ahead, and describing how you would like it to be. Of course, no one can predict the future, but you can use the exercise to create a direction for yourself. No matter how large or how small the plan, where you are going to end up is the key to being able to fill in the required steps in the middle. You need to be as specific as your imagination allows.

Again, write this vision down on paper. Ask yourself who you want to be when the plan has been executed properly. What new things did you want to learn about? What will your life look like? Examine these questions and describe your perfect future like you truly believe in its reality.

Starting with the big picture will help you stay on the right path as you move on to the next step. It will also allow you to design your strategy along with a collection of more specific short-term plans to make your vision a reality.

Break It Down: Set Short-term Goals

"Most of us spend too much time on what is urgent and not enough time on what is important."
Stephen R. Covey

The third step in the process is understanding exactly how and what it will take for you to reach your end result. This is the "middle bit," or the actual work required in order to gain the next level of success you desire. To achieve universal alignment, you must be willing to put in the time and effort, and this is the right place to do that.

This step of the planning process contains two parts. With your vision in mind, first you need to outline a strategy for reaching your long-term goals. This part is about figuring out how things need to be done and honestly evaluating the resources available to you. Ask yourself the following three questions:

- How will you get there?
- What resources are currently available to you?
- What do you "need" in order to move toward your end result?

For example, if I were an entrepreneur and my vision was to offer my services beyond my physical location, my strategy may be to create a website within a year. I also may find that my current resources are limited because I know very little about web development. Then what I would need is a professional web designer to help me with my website.

The second part of this step involves short-term goal setting. This is where you set Specific, Measureable, Attainable, Realistic, and Temporal (SMART) goals for the next three to six months to implement your strategy.

Using the same entrepreneur example above, my short-term goal may be to interview three web designers within ninety days and select one to complete my website.

As long as you stay in touch with your purpose and vision in life, the logical simplicity of this process can be repeated for all areas of your life—from health and fitness to personal development, relationships, or personal finance.

Start the Journey: Turn Action into Habit

"To do is to be." - Socrates

Earlier in this book I talked about the importance of taking action and referred to action as the engine of experience. In this step of the planning process, the objective is to make taking appropriate action habitual in your life. You can achieve this through commitment and diligence to your plans.

The actual journey of doing the work, implementing a plan, and realizing the rewards helps you form effective, actionable habits. The more you do, the more it becomes like second nature to you. In his book, *The Power of Habit*, Charles Duhigg says: *"Champions don't do extraordinary things. They do ordinary things, but they do them without thinking, too fast for the other team to react. They follow the habits they've learned."*

If the planning has been done properly, you should be able to trace the significance of every action on your daily, weekly, or monthly to-do list to your vision and your mission in life. Your plans should include things that you are passionate about, and you should be functioning in an environment of positive empowering perspectives.

To help increase your diligence and make "getting things done" a life-long habit:

- Review your alignment daily (passion, perspective, purpose, planning).
- Review your goals daily
- Take daily action and execute with conviction.

Do not allow yourself to slip into inactivity. Keeping all these elements aligned will make executing your plans a much more habitual process.

Evaluate: Do More of What Works and Change What Doesn't

"Insanity: doing the same thing over and over again and expecting different results."
Albert Einstein

When you make plans, sometimes they succeed and sometimes they fail. This is just what happens. If everything worked all of the time, we would all be wildly successful. Instead, we are given the opportunity to learn how to improve our planning ability. This is achieved by evaluating, redefining, and then re-implementing your plans. How else do you expect to know the effects but to measure the results? There will always be tangible and intangible results that you have to sort through.

In other words, you need an evaluation system for all your existing plans. It should run concurrently and be something that you work on often. Take notes on the positive and the negative results. Believe me, there will be plenty of both! The key is to identify and do more of what is working and change your approach when things are not going according to plans.

As the step that completes the planning loop, an effective evaluation system will shine a light on limitations and opportunities within your plans. It will help you answer questions like—how can it be improved? Where did I go wrong? Is there a way to get the same results in a faster manner?

Through this step of the planning process, you will gain the knowledge to optimize your plans and move forward with deeper insight and the solid strength of experience.

STEP 5

Progress

LEADING A LIFE OF PROGRESS

"Success is steady progress toward one's personal goals."
JIM ROHN

The final step along your universal alignment path is to continue to advance toward your goals, your vision, and ultimately your life-long purpose. Progress is about ongoing growth and leveraging what you have been learning to continuously measure your results, adjust your approach if things do not work, and celebrate your success when things go right.

Indecision Is the Enemy

"Iron rusts from disuse; water loses its purity from stagnation…even so does inaction sap the vigor of the mind."
Leonardo da Vinci

Since you are reading this book, you have obviously decided to make a change in your life. By doing so, you have overcome the greatest enemy of progress—indecision.

Indecisiveness leads to stagnation, and it is not human nature to be stagnant. Our souls are like water; movement keeps the water powerful and curious. Stagnation, on the other hand, makes the water murky and full of debris. No one wants a murky soul!

Making a decision is the starting point in living a better life. It is the step before taking action. Once you make a decision to do something, you have taken the first step in your journey. Even if it leads to a less than ideal situation, it is better than being indecisive. It gives you a chance to enjoy new experiences and use your empowering perspectives to maximize the outcome regardless of what it is.

Make a decision—it could be the most powerful tool you have at your disposal.

Do Not Be Left with Unrealized Potential

"Poor is the pupil that does not surpass his master."
Leonardo da Vinci

Leonardo da Vinci was an eccentric visionary who knew the key to a balanced life was constant forward progression. In many ways, he feverishly pursued progress in a way that many of his contemporaries failed to understand.

The quote above is credited to what da Vinci experienced when he teamed up with his master, Verrocchio, on a painting in Florence. When Verrocchio saw the angel da Vinci had painted, he put down his brushes and never painted again. Such was the force of progress in da Vinci's work.

Part of making progress is absolutely doing your best once you have decided to do something. You must strive and not be left with unrealized potential. Leaving your abilities untapped will be a great source of frustration.

You can help shape your life, and it is your responsibility to be the best you can be so your gifts and talents make it into the world. If you do not use what you have been given, it will fall away or waste away, and that is a great failure.

Persistence is what you should have for your goals and plans in life. Things will not move forward on their own; if you allow it, they will stagnate. You must be willing to apply yourself and fight hard for progress.

An Accurate Definition of Progress

Progress can be simply defined as forward movement toward a destination. You should already know you are on a journey meant for great things. After all, your soul is connected to the universal consciousness that runs through every living being on this planet. It is absolutely your duty to continue to reach for greater levels of personal and universal growth.

In order to move forward, you need reinforcement. I think progress is about creating and maintaining inspiration for this forward movement. I define progress as the engine of inspiration.

Albert Einstein said, *"Life is like riding a bicycle. To keep your balance, you must keep moving."* In the same way, to maintain universal alignment, you must continue to push through your boundaries and limits.

Progress will provide the inspiration you need to keep you going. When you combine it with the other universal elements, it makes a perfect closed loop, is a complete recipe for growth, and leads to fulfillment and happiness. Keep all five elements of the universal alignment in check, and make progress a lifestyle.

How Life and Progress Are Linked

"Our lifestyle communicates a clear message about who we are and what we think."
Jim Rohn

If we agree that progress is the engine of inspiration and that we need inspiration to keep us motivated in moving forward, then making progress must become a lifestyle. It must become our way of thinking—an automatic expectation in life. That is the link between life and progress.

How to Make Progress a Lifestyle

In many ways, this book is really about using the first four elements of passion, perspective, purpose, and planning to create a life of progress for yourself. The connection between these elements boils down to harnessing the forces within you to live a happier and more fulfilling life. Here are a few steps to help make progress a lifestyle:

1. *Awareness* – Realize that progress is the engine of inspiration and that you need inspiration to move forward. Look for opportunities to be inspired.

2. *Decisiveness* – Take action. This is the only way to experience things in life. With the right perspective, all results help you learn and make progress.

3. *Persistence* – Absolutely do your best. There is no inspiration in doing something without commitment.

4. *Measurement* – Keep track of your progress. Things that are measured have the best chance of improving.

5. *Celebration* – Enjoy your accomplishments. They are a great source of inspiration and help in making progress a habit.

We have already touched on the first three steps, and we will discuss the other two steps next. All these steps help you increase the level of inspiration in your life which can directly enhance your level of commitment and desire.

Measuring Your Life Progress

"What's measured improves." Peter F. Drucker

The business world often learns from everyday living virtues and experiences. For example, you frequently see professional sports coaches used as motivational speakers at business conventions. On the contrary, one thing that we could learn from both business and sports is leveraging measurement to improve performance and progress in our everyday life.

Measurement, of course, is always done to help maximize our effort in our quest to achieve our goals by figuring out what is working in order to do more of it and what is not working in order to change. However, the actual act of measurement itself has two basic parts—what to measure and how often to measure.

To help us measure our progress in life, we can learn from what works in the business world. In business, you often need to determine your Key Performance Indicators, commonly known as KPIs. This is where you determine what and when exactly to measure in order to see if your strategies are running along the right path. You also can use this technique in your life to ensure you are hitting your goals and progressing toward your purpose.

For example, a logical KPI for your simple goal of saving $1,000 in six months in a vacation account would be the "amount saved." This is the "what to measure," and since you know you can contribute to this account on a monthly basis, you make note of your progress at the end of each month. This would be the "how often to measure" factor.

The best time to determine what and how often to measure is during the planning process and the goal setting activity. But no matter what method you use, measuring your progress is essential to generating inspiration and keeping you on track for achieving a life of balance and fulfillment.

Celebrating Progress in Life

"Every moment and every event of every man's life on earth plants something in his soul."
Thomas Merton

You celebrate your birthday, anniversaries, and holidays—so why not celebrate when you achieve real progress in life? Especially since celebrating progress is a chance to generate a burst of inspiration for you. We are often too quick to dismiss this opportunity.

Imagine that you have an account, much like you would at a bank, except that what you deposit into this account is inspiration, not money. You would draw from this account when you need motivation to make a decision, take an action, and achieve a goal. Obviously, the more you deposit, the more you have to withdraw. Celebrating progress is a powerful way of making deposits into this account.

Another important aspect of celebrating progress is to not just celebrate your own progress. It is as much of an inspiration to acknowledge and genuinely be happy for the achievements of others. We are all connected; allow yourself to be inspired by others. This draws directly to having a positively empowering perspective about others.

If you have made it this far in this book, my hope is that you can see the connection between all of the five elements in the action cycle and the role of inspiration in your life. Let's examine the "Action Cycle" one more time.

The Action Cycle

This cycle involves all five of the universal elements. By recognizing your purpose and passion, you will be able to plan, which leads to actionable, step-by-step instructions for your life goals. Taking action leads to results—either success or failure. With the right perspective, you will be able to keep yourself inspired and move back and forth from the planning stage, never settling and always living a life of progress.

In this way, you will universally align yourself and achieve unprecedented levels of happiness in every aspect of your life.

You have the potential; you have the universal formula. Now get out there and start living an aligned life!

FIVE STEPS TO GREATER PERSONAL ENLIGHTENMENT

"Putting pen to paper lights more fire than matches ever will."
MALCOLM S. FORBES

I think it is extremely important for you to write down your take on the ideas and the concepts discussed in this book. Committing your thoughts and plans to paper will help create clarity, motivation, and focus.

In the following sections, I have outlined the five elements in this book along with some guiding questions to help you put together a journal of your discoveries.

My hope is that you commit yourself to going through the different sections and recording your answers as you embark on this alignment journey with me.

The Passion Checklist

Definition: Passion is a form of energy. It is discovered through life's experiences, and it is cultivated through practice.

Ways to Discover Passion

- *Look back at past experiences to answer these questions:*
  - ○ What mattered most to you as a child?
  - ○ What did you love then, and what do you love now?
  - ○ What were your dreams, and what are they now?
  - ○ Who did you enjoy being around?
  - ○ What did you find most beautiful in this world?
  - ○ If you had it all, what would you still be doing?

- *Examine your current life and answer these questions:*
  - ○ Where do you lose yourself?
  - ○ Which activities steal hours from your day?
  - ○ Are these activities positive in nature?
  - ○ Which activities do you want to return to again and again?
  - ○ Do you think about the activities often?
  - ○ Do you wish you could be doing the activity all the time?

- *Examine the areas of your natural focus:*
  - ○ Where in your life are you the most focused?
  - ○ What do you focus on?
  - ○ What is the focus like? Is it forced or effortless?
  - ○ How do you feel when you are focused?

Ways to Practice Passion

- Make time for what you love to do.
- Never stop discovering and exploring new experiences.
- Learn all you can about your discovered passion.
- Inspire others to seek happiness through their passion.

Lesson: *Passion is personal and from your very core. It must be discovered and practiced!*

The Perspective Checklist

Definition: Perspective is the driving force behind all actions that shape your personal universe. It has a pivotal role in your life, and it is always a choice.

Ways to Develop Empowering Perspectives

- *Describe your perspective on all five key areas:*
    - ° Your Universal Perspective
    - ° Your Self Perspective
    - ° Your Perspective about Others
    - ° Your Perspective of Events and Circumstances
    - ° Your Perspective about Money and Worldly Possessions

- *Adjust your descriptions until the answer to the following questions is a solid "Yes" for all five areas.*
    - ° Is your perspective positive?
    - ° Is your perspective empowering?

Lesson: *Perspective is central to all of your actions. It must be understood and optimized for positive empowerment!*

The Purpose Checklist

Definition: Your purpose in life is the universe's core reason for your existence in relation to all other things that exist. It comes from a higher source, and it is your mission in life.

Ways to Write a Purpose Statement

- *Find the common thread in the answer to these questions:*
    - ° What attracts you, engages you, and fires up your heart?
    - ° Given a choice, what do you want to do every single day?
    - ° What in the world would you like to contribute to in a positive manner?

- ° What do you want to be remembered for?
- ° What activity, work or non-work related, brings you the most satisfaction?
- ° What was the happiest day of your life? Why? What about you and your values has been affirmed by this insight?
- ° What was the worst day of your life? Why? What was trampled on?
- ° If you could change one thing about the world and what we experience by being here, what would it be?

Test Your Purpose Statement

- *Examine your purpose statement to make sure it has the following characteristics:*
  - ° It serves the "greater good."
  - ° It benefits more than just you.
  - ° It has no time limits.
  - ° It is not about money and material things.

Ways to Embrace Your Purpose

- Review your purpose statement regularly.
- Stay committed to your purpose.
- Share your purpose with others.
- Respect the purpose of others.
- Plan in alignment with your purpose.

Lesson: *Purpose is universal and from a higher source. It must be recognized and embraced!*

The Planning Checklist

Definition: A plan is a fluid map of actions—a map because it provides a direction and fluid because it requires flexibility through the journey.

Ways to Develop a Planning Mind-set

- Be prepared to take action.
- Practice deliberate patience.
- Utilize the other elements when planning:
  - Leverage your passion within your plan.
  - Employ your empowering perspectives.
  - Ensure that all your goals and actions get you closer to achieving your life-long purpose.
- Set goals that pass the SMART test, which means they must be **S**pecific, **M**easurable, **A**chievable, **R**elevant, and **T**emporal.

For example: Do not say, "I want to be rich." Say, "I want to earn an additional $200.00 by Wednesday on my website." This goal passes the SMART test.

Steps in the Planning Process:

- *Get real: Where are you now?*
  - Describe your current situation.
  - What is currently working?
  - What is not currently working?

- *Imagine a vision: Set long-term goals.*
  - Describe your ideal situation in three to five years.
  - Describe your ideal situation in one year.
  - List as many reasons as you can about why you must create these ideal situations.
  - List strategies you can use to realize your vision.
  - List resources available to you and the additional resources you will need.
  - Make sure your long-term goals are SMART.

- *Break it down: Set short-term goals.*
  - ○ Think smaller goals within a three to six month period
  - ○ List detailed short-term goals to achieve.
  - ○ Make sure your short-term goals are SMART.
  - ○ Prioritize the action list.
  - ○ Review your goals daily.

- *Start the journey: Turn action into habit.*
  - ○ Review your alignment daily (passion, perspective, purpose, planning).
  - ○ Take daily action.
  - ○ Execute your plans with conviction.

- *Evaluate: Do more of what works, and change what does not. Seek to achieve this purpose by making a solid plan!*
  - ○ Review your goals every day.
  - ○ What is working? Do more of it.
  - ○ What is not working? Change it.

Lesson: *Planning is a fluid map of actions that leads to events. It must be aligned with your life-long purpose!*

The Progress Checklist

Definition: Progress is the engine of inspiration. It provides the motivation necessary for forward movement in life.

Ways to Make Progress a Lifestyle

- *Look for opportunities to inspire and to be inspired.*
  - ○ What inspires you?
  - ○ How can you inspire others?

- *Decide to take action.*
  - ○ What area of your life needs improvement?
  - ○ What can you do today to improve it?

- ° How would this change your life?

- *Absolutely do your best.*
  - ° Why do you have to improve your life?
  - ° What would be the results of inaction?
  - ° How would you feel if you do not live up to your potential?

- *Measure your results to recognize success.*
  - ° What will you measure?
  - ° How often will you measure?

- *Celebrate your achievements.*
  - ° What accomplishments of your own or of others can you celebrate?
  - ° How will you celebrate these accomplishments?

Lesson: *Progress is the engine of inspiration. It must be measured, celebrated, and utilized for it to become a lifestyle!*

Achieving Universal Balance and Alignment

They say that life is a journey, and it is—only we are more in control of the quality of this journey than we think. Each of us has a purpose that we must faithfully embrace if we ever hope to feel fulfilled and happy. When you achieve universal balance and alignment, amazing things happen. Not only do you outperform what you think you can handle but you achieve things you never believed possible.

Universal alignment will help awaken you and lead you to a more purpose-driven life. Your life should be filled with goodness and reward, and it should be celebrated often. Only when you give yourself over to the five elements will this happen.

- Discover your passions.
- Adjust your perspectives.
- Recognize your life's purpose.

- Create aligned goals and plans.
- Live a life of progress.

These elements are all related to the universe and how it works by design. Chi, karma, the forces of nature, the human spirit—there is still so much we do not understand. But I think life is about finding that understanding through our positive actions. That is how you achieve balance. You will be tested, and there will be obstacles. But if you want success, balance, happiness, and fulfillment, you have to be prepared to work for it.

I have provided you with the path to a richer life; now it is up to you to take the steps!

Conclusion

"If you want to awaken all of humanity, then awaken all of yourself. If you want to eliminate the suffering in the world, then eliminate all that is dark and negative in yourself. Truly, the greatest gift you have to give is that of your own self-transformation."
LAO TZU

Thank you for journeying through this book with me and for considering my words in relation to your own life. I cannot wait until you begin to practice these five elements so that you can achieve the universal alignment you so deserve.

When you take the time to align yourself with who you are, what you want, and why you were put here on this earth, everything makes a little more sense. There is real peace in finding a meaningful purpose in life.

Please remember that life works in twos. There is balance, Yin and Yang, right and wrong, active or passive. If you choose to ignore the lessons in this book, you are choosing to walk away from the opportunity to find real balance in your hectic life. So I urge you—do not forget these words. Do not stop practicing passion, perspective, purpose, planning, and progress. This is the universal blueprint that can help you find out who you are among all the other stars in the universe.

I hope this book acts as your starting point and convinces you of your limitless possibilities when you are in perfect alignment with who you are and what your role is in respect to others.

Change is a certainty. By applying balance in your life, you will change for the better—and maybe, just maybe, you will also end up changing the world for the better too.

Wishing you every success in your journey,

Farzin (Frank) Kamal

References

Chapter 1

Hill, Napoleon, *Brainy Quote*, http://www.brainyquote.com/quotes/quotes/n/napoleonhi131107.html

Magsamen, Sandra, *Live Your Passion*, http://www.oprah.com/spirit/Live-Your-Passion

Edison, Thomas A, *Brainy Quote*, http://www.brainyquote.com/quotes/quotes/t/thomasaed149059.html

Davenport, Barrie, *15 Tiny Action to Strip Yourself Bare and Reveal Your Passion*, http://liveboldandbloom.com/11/career/15-tiny-actions-to-strip-yourself-bare-and-reveal-your-passion

Friend, Jeffrey, *6 Ways To Live a Life of Passion and Adventure Right Now*, http://tinybuddha.com/blog/6-ways-to-live-a-life-of-passion-and-adventure-right-now/

Chapter 2

Bernstein, Gabrielle, *How To Follow Your Passion When You're Just Trying To Pay The Bills*, http://www.huffingtonpost.com/gabrielle-bernstein/passion-career_b_1209046.html

Girard, Lisa, *Five Creativity Exercises To Find Your Passion*, http://www.entrepreneur.com/article/219709

Anderson, Erika, *3 Simple Ways To Discover Your Passion*, http://www.forbes.com/sites/erikaandersen/2012/07/23/3-simple-ways-to-discover-your-passion/

Babauta, Leo, *The Short But Powerful Guide To Finding Your Passion*, http://zenhabits.net/the-short-but-powerful-guide-to-finding-your-passion/

Chapter 3

Gandhi, Mahatma, *Brainy Quote,* http://www.brainyquote.com/quotes/quotes/m/mahatmagan125863.html

Edison, Thomas A, *Wikiquote,* http://en.wikiquote.org/wiki/Thomas_Edison

Tao Te Ching 2003, *A Definitive Edition.* (Jonathan Starr). New York, NY: Tracher.

Churchill, Winston, *Brainy Quote,* http://www.brainyquote.com/quotes/quotes/w/winstonchu138235.html

James, William, *Brainy Quote,* http://www.brainyquote.com/quotes/quotes/w/williamjam107172.html

Allsopp, Glen, *Two Questions To Help You Gain Perspective*, http://zenhabits.net/two-questions-to-help-you-gain-perspective/

Babauta, Leo, *39 Ways To Live, and Not Merely Exist*, http://www.altering-perspectives.com/2013/06/39-ways-to-live-and-not-merely-exist.html

Maloney, Cheryl, *Perspective By Choice*, http://simplestepsrealchange.com/2013/05/17/perspective-by-choice/

Holland, Janet, Thomson, Rachel, *Gaining a Perspective a Choice and Fate: Revising Critical Moments*, http://oro.open.ac.uk/19641/

Chapter 4

Lincoln, Abraham, *Goodreads*, http://www.goodreads.com/quotes/67318-we-can-complain-because-rose-bushes-have-thorns-or-rejoice

Gandhi, Mahatma, *Brainy Quote,* http://www.brainyquote.com/quotes/quotes/m/mahatmagan160715.html

Satir, Virginia, *Thinkexist.com* http://thinkexist.com/quotation/we_must_not_allow_other_people-s_limited/171657.htm

Estep, Eliot, *Healer Demonstrates Extraordinary Power of Chi, Battles Scientists*, http://www.collective-evolution.com/2013/07/19/healer-demonstrates-extraordinary-powers-of-chi/#_

Hill, Napoleon, *Auto-Suggestion,* http://www.sacred-texts.com/nth/tgr/tgr09.htm

Edberg, Henrik, *Gandhi's Top 10 Fundamentals for Changing the World,* http://www.positivityblog.com/index.php/2008/05/09/gandhis-top-10-fundamentals-for-changing-the-world

Mandela, Nelson, *Brainyquote,* http://www.brainyquote.com/quotes/quotes/n/nelsonmand178791.html

Dr. Sarkis, Stephanie, *50 Quotes on Perspective,* http://www.psychologytoday.com/blog/here-there-and-everywhere/201210/50-quotes-perspective

Kotsos, Tania, *You Are One With The Universal Mind,* http://www.mind-your-reality.com/universal_mind.html

Braden, Gregg, *Is The Inner World – The Real World?,* http://www.one-mind-one-energy.com/innerworld.html

Steiner, Rudolf, *The Human Soul and The Universe,* http://wn.rsarchive.org/Lectures/19170220p02.html

Chapter 5

Buddha, *Tinybuddha,* http://tinybuddha.com/wisdom-quotes/your-work-is-to-discover-your-world-and-then-with-all-your-heart-give-yourself-to-it/

Owen, Wilfred, *Goodquotes,* http://www.goodquotes.com/quote/wilfred-owen/i-was-a-boy-when-i-first-realized-that

Pavlina, Steve, *How To Discover Your Life Purpose in About 20 Minutes,* http://www.stevepavlina.com/blog/2005/01/how-to-discover-your-life-purpose-in-about-20-minutes/

Mandela, Nelson, *Brainyquote,* http://www.brainyquote.com/quotes/quotes/n/nelsonmand391070.html

Einstein, Albert, *The World As I See It,* http://www.aip.org/history/einstein/essay.htm

Gandhi, Mahatma, *Brainyquote,* http://www.brainyquote.com/quotes/quotes/m/mahatmagan105686.html

Brillianceaudio. (2012, April 10). *How to Develop Your Personal Mission Statement by Stephen R. Covey.* Retrieved from http://www.youtube.com/watch?v=E90Z5HQwtGY

Novalis, *Brainyquote,* http://www.brainyquote.com/quotes/quotes/n/novalis383599.html

Kennedy, Robert F. *Goodreads,* http://www.goodreads.com/quotes/145501-the-purpose-of-life-is-to-contribute-in-some-way

Gandhi, Mahatma. *Goodreads,* http://www.goodreads.com/quotes/2253-live-as-if-you-were-to-die-tomorrow-learn-as

Dr. Klontz, Brad, *Mind Over Money,* http://www.psychologytoday.com/blog/mind-over-money/201309/living-purpose

Sokol, Jacob, *7 Ways To Tell That You're Not Living Your Highest Purpose in Life (And 7 Tricks For Fixing That),* http://www.sensophy.com/how-to-live-your-highest-purpose-in-life/

Chapter 6

Purpose Quotes, *Brainy Quote,* http://www.brainyquote.com/quotes/keywords/purpose.html

Purpose of Life, *Spiritual Science Research Foundation,* http://www.spiritualresearchfoundation.org/articles/id/spiritualresearch/spiritualscience/purposeoflife

Dr. Dyer, Wayne, *What's My Purpose in Life?,* http://www.healyourlife.com/author-dr-wayne-w-dyer/2013/04/wisdom/inspiration/whats-my-life-purpose

Buddha, *Buddhanet,net,* The teacher of Gods and men, http://www.buddhanet.net/e-learning/buddhism/disciples06.htm

Einstein, Albert, *Brainyquote,* http://www.brainyquote.com/quotes/quotes/a/alberteins145936.html

Mandela, Nelson, *Goodreads,* http://www.goodreads.com/quotes/570856-we-must-use-time-wisely-and-forever-realize-that-the

Lao Tzu, *Goodreads,* http://www.goodreads.com/quotes/20370-to-understand-the-limitation-of-things-desire-them

Lumbila, Campbell, *Discover & Embrace Your Purpose,* http://www.motivation-for-dreamers.com/discover-embrace-your-purpose.html

Keller, Helen, *Brainyquotes,* http://www.brainyquote.com/quotes/quotes/h/helenkelle386922.html

Chapter 7

Lincoln, Abraham, *Goodreads,* http://www.goodreads.com/quotes/83633-give-me-six-hours-to-chop-down-a-tree-and

Franklin, Bejamin, *Brainy Quote,* http://www.brainyquote.com/quotes/quotes/b/benjaminfr138217.html

Thum, Myrko, *Top 10 Inspiring Lao Tzu Quotes,* http://www.myrkothum.com/top-10-most-inspiring-quotes-of-lao-tzu/

Hill, Napoleon, *Brainy Quote,* http://www.brainyquote.com/quotes/quotes/n/napoleonhi152837.html

Lao Tzu, *Goodreads,* http://www.goodreads.com/quotes/341604-do-you-have-the-patience-to-wait-till-your-mud

Reninger, Elizabeth , *About.com, Wu Wei: the Action of Non-Action,* http://taoism.about.com/od/wuwei/a/wuwei.htm

Why Set Goals?, http://www.goalmaker.com/whyset.html

Lao Tzu Quotes, *Brainy Quote,* http://www.brainyquote.com/quotes/authors/l/lao_tzu.html

What Is Planning and Why You Need To Plan, http://www.techrepublic.com/resource-library/whitepapers/what-is-planning-and-why-you-need-to-plan/

Lieff, SJ, *Perspective: The Missing Link in Academic Career Planning and Development: Pursuit of Meaningful and Aligned Work,* http://www.ncbi.nlm.nih.gov/pubmed/19881426

Brown Paul B, *How To Plan Your Life, When You Can't Plan Your Life,* http://www.forbes.com/sites/actiontrumpseverything/2013/01/13/how-to-plan-your-life-when-you-cant-plan-your-life/

Chapter 8

Hill, Napoleon, *Goodreads*, http://www.goodreads.com/quotes/180743-set-your-mind-on-a-definite-goal-and-observe-how

Dr. Dyer, Wayne. W (2005). *The power of intention, Learning to create your world your way*, Californnia: Hey House.

Covey, Stephen R. (1989). *The 7 habits of highly effective people, Wisdom and insight from Stephen R.Covey*, New York, NY: Simon & Schuster.

Orman, Suze, *BrainyQuote,* http://www.brainyquote.com/quotes/quotes/s/suzeorman465792.html

Einstein, Albert, *Goodreads*, http://www.goodreads.com/quotes/tag/imagination

Bregman, Peter, *An 18-Minute Plan For Managing For Day*, http://blogs.hbr.org/2009/07/an-18minute-plan-for-managing/

Covey, Stephen R, *Goodreads*, http://www.goodreads.com/author/quotes/1538.Stephen_R_Covey

Planning Process, http://training.fema.gov/EMIWeb/is/ICSResource/assets/PlanningP.pdf

The Planning Cycle, MindTools, http://www.mindtools.com/pages/article/newPPM_05.htm

Creating SMART Goals, http://topachievement.com/smart.html

Setting Smart Management Goals, http://www.dummies.com/how-to/content/setting-smart-management-goals.html

Socrates, *Thinkexist,* http://thinkexist.com/quotation/to_do_is_to_be/149608.html

Duhigg, Charles (2012), *The Power of habit: Why we do what we do in life and business*, New York, NY: Random House.

Einstein, Albert, *BrainyQuote*, http://www.brainyquote.com/quotes/quotes/a/alberteins133991.html

Chapter 9

Rohn, Jim, *BrainyQuote,* http://www.brainyquote.com/quotes/quotes/j/jimrohn147514.html

da Vinci, Leonardo, *Thinkexist,* http://thinkexist.com/quotation/iron_rusts_from_disuse-water_loses_its_purity/14051.html

da Vinci, Leonardo, *Brainyquot,* http://www.brainyquote.com/quotes/quotes/l/leonardoda542476.html

Einstein, Albert, *Goodreads*, http://www.goodreads.com/quotes/29213-life-is-like-riding-a-bicycle-to-keep-your-balance

Guise, Stephen, *Your Life is Stagnant – Get Shock Treatment*, http://deepexistence.com/your-life-is-stagnant-get-shock-treatment/

Rohn, Jim E. (2002), *The Five Major Pieces to The Life Puzzle*, St.Augustine, FL. Asamanthinketh.net.

Drucker, Peter F. *Goodreads*, http://www.goodreads.com/author/quotes/12008.Peter_F_Drucker

Measure Your Progress Toward Your Vision, http://www.amanet.org/training/articles/Measure-Your-Progress-Toward-Your-Vision.aspx

Merton, Thomas, *Brainyquote*, http://www.brainyquote.com/quotes/quotes/t/thomasmert385677

Nobbs, Michael, *Remember to Celebrate Your Achievements*, http://www.sustainablycreative.com/celebrate-your-achievements/

Chapter 10

Forbes, Malcolm S., *Goodreads,* http://www.goodreads.com/quotes/311685-putting-pen-to-paper-lights-more-fire-than-matches-ever

Writing SMART Goals, http://www.hr.virginia.edu/uploads/documents/media/Writing_SMART_Goals.pdf

Setting SMART Goals, http://www.lehigh.edu/~inhro/documents/SMART_GoalsHandout.pdf

Locke's Goal Setting Theory, http://www.mindtools.com/pages/article/newHTE_87.htm

Conclusion

Lao Tzu, *Goodreads*, http://www.goodreads.com/quotes/753949-if-you-want-to-awaken-all-of-humanity-then-awaken

About the Author

While much of Frank Kamal's skill and professional experience comes from working in positions such as an engineering manager and CEO, it is his sports training he credits for his start. His experience with athletics and coaching is where he first learned the importance of traits and habits for success such as working hard, being prepared, teamwork, adapting to unpredictable situations, and coping with the opposition. It was this kind of training that led to his career path and being chosen to lead a highly technical team at the young age of just twenty-nine.

Yet it was his entrepreneurship and owning his own business that helped Kamal gain so much knowledge about the world of business. There is a lot more to his career history that makes him qualified to be a life coach and write this book.

Kamal has held multiple senior executive and leadership positions in professional industries such as sales, marketing and overall strategic business planning.

He has also worked in diverse professional fields including sports apparel manufacturing, web development, ecommerce and mobile social networking, just to name a few. After having his own business, Kamal began his career in the world of business consulting. He quickly realized how gratifying this career choice was and how he seemed to have a natural knack in this industry. Being a Certified Professional Life Coach and continuing his passion for coaching youth soccer has been the most fulfilling part of Kamal's professional and personal journey.

Kamal also prides himself on the level of professional expertise he offers. Whether working with him as a consultant personally or another member of his consulting team, you get the best service possible. His main goal and driving force is to offer others important business consulting and life coaching advice that can help them find ultimate success.

When not working, he can be found studying a new concept, developing a new idea, spending time with friends and family or catching a live soccer match on TV.

For more information visit www.frankkamal.com

www.ingramcontent.com/pod-product-compliance
Lightning Source LLC
LaVergne TN
LVHW021538080426
835509LV00019B/2719